CATS

CATS

LUXURIOUS LOUNGERS

Kirsty Seymour-Ure

RYLAND
PETERS
& SMALL

LONDON NEW YORK

Senior Designer Paul Tilby
Editor Sophie Bevan
Editorial Assistant Miriam Hyslop
Location Research Manager Kate Brunt
Production Patricia Harrington
Art Director Gabriella Le Grazie
Publishing Director Alison Starling

Special Photography Chris Tubbs

First published in the United Kingdom in 2001
by Ryland Peters & Small
12–14 Whitfield Street, Kirkman House,
London W1T 2RP
www.rylandpeters.com

10 9 8 7 6 5 4 3

Text © Kirsty Seymour-Ure 2001
Design and photographs
© Ryland Peters & Small 2001

Printed and bound in China by
Toppan Printing Co.

The author's moral rights have been
asserted. All rights reserved. No part
of this publication may be reproduced,
stored in a retrieval system, or
transmitted in any form or by any
means, electronic, mechanical,
photocopying or otherwise,
without the prior permission of
the publisher.

ISBN 1 84172 125 5

A CIP record for this book is
available from the British Library.

contents

devoted
companions

In love and affection, as in everything, cats are choosy. The reward of a cat's friendship, once earned, is all the more special for not being so lightly given.

The ancient Egyptians were probably the first people to have kept cats as domestic animals - initially as mouse-catchers in the granaries, then doubtless yielding to their charms as household pets. They also held the cat sacred, worshipping it in the form of a cat-headed goddess named Bast. Sacred icon, beloved pet: a strange mixture perhaps, but one that makes it easy

CULT CATS

to see why cats consistently exert such fascination. In the steadfast gaze of our modern fireside friend do we perceive something of the inscrutable mystery that the Egyptians revered?

The cat has not changed very much for millions of years, and today's domestic cat retains many of the characteristics of the wild cat from which it is descended – as well as of its big-cat cousins such as the lion and tiger. Supremely agile, the cat moves with a fluid, sinuous grace, whether he is chasing after a bird, leaping for a piece of string, or simply strolling over to his bowl of milk. His perfect coordination, athletic ability and lightning reflexes are those of his wild relatives; unlike the big cats, however, this cat will never roar at you.

ANCIENT AND WILD

. . . such soft,
melting eyes,
such a human
and caressing
look . . . it seems
impossible that
reason can be
absent from it.

Théophile Gautier (1811–72)

The cat is playful yet haughty at the same time; she is both a soft, fluffy bundle of fun and an elegant, enigmatic sphinx of the hearth. She is so clearly superior to us and yet, miraculously, she deigns to live with us. The cat is our friend! We  are happy to give up our favourite old chair without so much as a murmur, in return for the pleasure of having a cat to stroke, a cat that loves us. The pleasure is beautifully reciprocal too, as expressed in the cat's unique purr, like a seal of friendship. What more can we ask than a cat that waits by the window and listens for our step in the street; a cat to come home to?

Cats have a celebrated independence of nature that makes their willing companionship all the more pleasing. You can't buy a cat's devotion – bribes don't work (although they are rarely refused). Offering affection and accepting love, a cat may choose to stay with you, but he remains a free spirit.

INDEPENDENT SPIRITS

sleek sloths

Cats love to sleep — they doze long and deeply, or take swift, refreshing catnaps. Few sights are as peaceful as a pair of sleek cats contentedly asleep.

Sixteen hours of a typical cat's day are spent asleep – more than any other mammal – and no one knows exactly why. Being hunters, they need to conserve their energy; but house cats hunt for fun, not survival. Yet still they sleep and they sleep! These languid, lazy hours may be important to a cat's well-being in some way not understood by us; we can only envy their ability to while away the day in serene indifference to the world.

SOUND ASLEEP

PERCHANCE TO DREAM

Do cats dream? We like to think so as we watch our pet cat twitch his ears, flick his tail, flex his claws and growl in his sleep. Is he dreaming of his next meal – and would that be the bowl of biscuits or the fresh-caught mouse? Even in deep sleep a part of the cat's brain is on constant red-alert, so that at the slightest sign of danger he is instantly wide awake. He will purr in his sleep at the caress of a hand, but in general a cat will not appreciate having his sleep disturbed – even by a loved owner, and even when he is on that owner's comfortable bed.

LAP OF LUXURY

However beautiful and stylish your house may be, it truly becomes a home when it has a cat living there. Rooms are softened, warmed and - strange to say - humanized by the presence of a cat. Cats do pretty well out of it too, especially if they are able to luxuriate on your best sheepskin or fur. They may be ruthless hunters when they choose, but cats are hedonists at heart, and rarely pass up a chance of indulging in some sensuous sleep fulfilment.

luxurious
loungers

Pedigree cats and long-haired breeds can seem rare and refined, as if born to a life of luxury and pampering, a life in which sleep, naturally, plays a prominent part.

Cats, of course, will sleep anywhere, and somehow they always find the best spot. A sun-soaked patch by the window allows them to be admired to the full, while a basket in front of a woodburning stove takes

LAZY DAYS

the chill off a stone-flagged kitchen floor. They doze in all the obvious places – on sofas, chairs and beds – but you are just as likely to find a cat relaxing in the laundry basket, on top of the CD player, at the back of the airing cupboard, or even in the bath.

The warm, soft, opulent fur of a cat is irresistibly strokable. What does it feel like? Thick cream. Expensive velvet. Fine wine. Stroking a cat is a wholly absorbing sensuous experience that goes far beyond the merely tactile. The cat curls and stretches in languid bliss under your repetitious hand, his purr rising and rising as he gives himself over to the sensation of being stroked. And as you smooth his rich, deep coat with the palm of your hand, you will find the stresses of your own day are gently soothed away.

Cunning, and old,
and sleek as jam.

William Brighty Rands (1823–82)

Black cats are traditionally associated with luck – good and bad – and with witchcraft. Not at all resembling creatures of Satan, however, long-haired pure black cats are striking, and seem purpose-designed to embellish whatever setting they have chosen to recline in.

on the prowl

The tiger that lurks beneath the skin needs little pretext to leap forth; our fireside feline can transform almost instantly into a finely honed hunting machine.

Cats are hunters, and they like to remember they are. Stalking a leaf, chasing a ping-pong ball, or pouncing on our shoelaces - all are the most serious of games.

A JUNGLE OUT THERE

45

Even well-fed, contented cats hunt: the instinct has not been suppressed with the millennia of domestication. The suddenness with which a cat can turn from a tame to a wild thing is surely part of its appeal. Those plush paws that sweetly pad across our floor are the same paws that, razor claws unsheathed, rake the mouse with such deadly intent. A cat's body is designed precisely for the stealthy creep and final sprint that are the essence of its hunting technique, while the intense, still concentration of a cat after its prey is awe-inspiring. If you are lucky and your cat wants to please, she will bring her prize to you as a present – an honour you would be careless to reject.

out of curiosity

The curiosity of cats is legendary. It leads them astray, entices them to mischief, gets them into trouble. It also brings out some of their most endearing moments.

Many places are intriguing to cats, including open drawers, high shelves, empty cardboard boxes, junk-filled garden sheds, and ill-lit cellars with no alternative exit. A partly open door is completely irresistible; the cat strolls through absolutely and happily single-minded in its desire to know

DICING WITH DOGS

what lies on the other side, the idea of danger or problems never entering its head. To turn round and find the door slammed shut behind it or its way blocked by the unexpected presence of a large dog is astonishing. How in the world could this have happened?

Cats may have the alleged nine lives, or they may even have more. What is certain is that they need them all. Their desire to investigate, reinforced by a sure sense of their own immortality and a certain devil-may-care attitude, leads them first into mischief and then, frequently, into hazardous situations. Their agility, together with the speed of their reflexes, is literally their saving grace, as they spring back from danger or twist in mid-air. Cats really do land on their feet.

... walking by his wild lone

Rudyard Kipling (1865–1936)

Paw prints on the kitchen table are an inevitable result of keeping a cat, as cats, although perfectly able to understand 'Bad kitty', are disinclined to obedience, especially when a slice of cake or buttered scone is a possibility. Getting their head stuck in the banisters, likewise, is no disincentive to curiosity.

The cat's gaze, eloquent, inquiring and with that hint of enigma, urges us to believe that her powers of perception are greater and deeper than ours. A cat will bristle and glare at a spot on the wall when we can see nothing.

THE SIXTH SENSE

Moreover, her ability to select and sit on the exact paragraph of the paper that we are reading is truly uncanny.

CREDITS

t=top, b=bottom, l=left, r=right

ALL PHOTOGRAPHY BY CHRIS TUBBS UNLESS OTHERWISE STATED

Endpapers photo Francesca Yorke; **1** Thin; **2** Georgie; **3** Button; **4–5** Claude; **6** Button; **9** photo Francesca Yorke; **10** Hyde; **12–13** Thin; **14** Gramercy; **15tl and tr** Georgie; **15bl** Sooty; **15br** Dennis; **16** Georgie; **17** China; **18 & 19** Georgie; **20** photo Polly Wreford/Ros Fairman's house in London; **23** photo Polly Wreford/Ann Shore's house in London; **24–25** photo Andrew Wood/Apartment of Michel Hurst/Robert Swope, owners of Full House NYC; **26** Sooty; **28** Thin; **29** photo Andrew Wood/Guido Palau's house in North London designed by Azman Owens Architects; **30** photo Andrew Wood/ Gabriele Sanders' house in New York; **33** photo Tom Leighton/Roger Oates and Fay Morgan's house in Hereforshire; **34** photo Polly Wreford/Ann Shore's house in London; **35** photo Chris Everard; **36** Dennis; **37** China; **38 & 39** photo Andrew Wood/Gabriele Sanders' house in New York; **40** Sooty; **43** Gramercy; **44** Pipkin; **45** Sooty; **46 and 47r** Coco; **47l** Thin; **49** Coco; **50** Claude; **53** Gramercy; **54** Button; **56–57** Claude; **58l** Coco; **58tr** Pipkin; **58 br** Georgie; **59** Coco; **60** Hyde and Gramercy; **61** China; **63l & br** Button; **63tr** Hyde.

The publisher would like to thank everyone
who allowed us to photograph their cats.
Special thanks to Elsa, Zia, Clare and Jamie,
Kristi and Ollie, Debbie and John, and Siobhan.